PET CARE

CATS

BY KATHRYN STEVENS

![The Child's World]

Published by The Child's World®
1980 Lookout Drive • Mankato, MN 56003-1705
800-599-READ • www.childsworld.com

Acknowledgments
The Child's World®: Mary Berendes, Publishing Director
The Design Lab: Design
Michael Miller: Editing
Sarah Miller: Editing

Photo Credits
© AngiePhotos/iStockphoto.com: 9; deepblue4you/iStockphoto.com:
7; Devonyu/iStockphoto.com: 12; Dreamframer/iStockphoto.com:
14-15; emyerson/iStockphoto.com: cover, 2, 6, 20 (cat food); enduro/
iStockphoto.com: 13; FrankvandenBergh/iStockphoto.com: 3, 16, 23
(mouse); gsermek/iStockphoto.com: 17; jgroup/iStockphoto.com: 15;
kamkar/iStockphoto.com: 20 (brush); PhotoDisc: back cover, cover, 2,
5, 19, 21, 22, 24; pio3/Shutterstock.com: cover (main), 1; princessdlaf/
iStockphoto.com: 10; SondraP/iStockphoto.com: 3, 23 (catnip);
Thomas_EyeDesign/iStockphoto.com: 8; Viktor Levi/Dreamstime.com:
4-5; Watcha/iStockphoto.com: 16 (feathers); Wildroze/iStockphoto.com:
18; w-ings/iStock[hptp.com: 11

ISBN: 9781631437267
LCCN: 2014959772

Printed in the United States of America
Mankato, MN
March, 2016
PA02312

NOTE TO PARENTS AND EDUCATORS

This Pet Care series is written for children who want
to be part of the pet experience but are too young
to be in charge of pets without adult supervision.
These books are intended to provide a kid-friendly
supplement to more detailed information adults
need to know about choosing and caring for
different types of pets. Adults can help youngsters
learn how to live happily with the animals in their
lives and, with adults' help and supervision, can
grow into responsible animal caretakers later on.

PET CARE

CONTENTS

CATS AS PETS

Lots of cats need good homes. And cats can make wonderful pets! But getting a cat is a big decision. Cats can live for a long time. They live for up to 20 years. They need people who will care for them the whole time.

This cat is 16 years old. She has lived with the same family the whole time.

This kitten is only a few weeks old. She needs people who will care for her for many years.

GOOD FOOD

Cats need good food to keep them healthy and strong. Crunchy dried cat food is good for cats' teeth. Cats love juicy, smelly canned food, too! Cats also need clean water to drink.

Crunchy dried food keeps cats' teeth clean.

This cat is enjoying some smelly, fishy cat food. Cats love the smell and taste of fish!

7

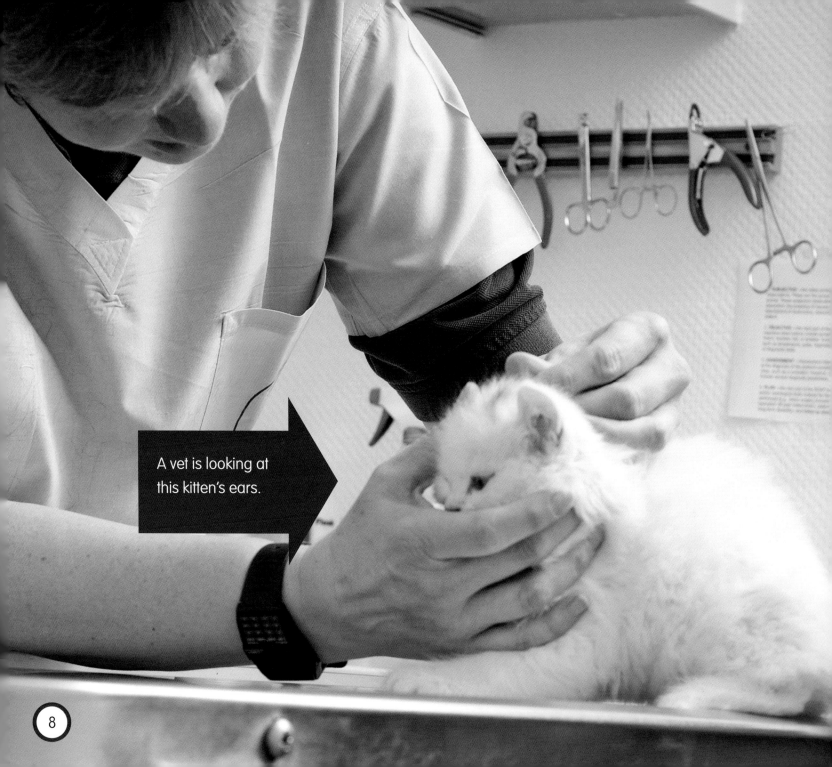

A vet is looking at this kitten's ears.

GOOD HEALTH

Cats need visits to an animal doctor, or **vet**. The vet makes sure the cat is healthy. The vet also gives shots to keep the cat from getting sick. Cats like to keep themselves clean. They lick their fur to clean it. Long-haired cats need **grooming**.

This cat is cleaning her paw.

Cats have sharp claws. They like to scratch on things. A scratching post keeps them from scratching the furniture. Indoor cats also need a place to go to the bathroom. They use a box filled with **litter**. The litter box should be cleaned every day.

This cat has a nice, clean litter box.

Scratching posts come in many shapes and sizes.

SAFETY

Cats that live outside face many dangers. They can get hurt or sick. Indoor cats live longer, safer lives. But they need to be kept safe, too. They need to be handled gently. They must be kept from things that could hurt them.

Eating rubber bands can make cats very sick.

This kitten loves playing with yarn. But eating it could harm her.

Cats are very **curious**. They love to explore. But exploring can get them into trouble. Sometimes they crawl into small places. Sometimes they climb too high. Then they can get stuck!

This cat climbed way up in a tree. Now he cannot get down.

Cats love to crawl into paper bags.

PLAYTIME

Kittens love to play. Many adult cats like to play, too. Cats like to pretend they are hunting. They sneak up on toys. They chase the toys and jump on them. They bat the toys with their paws. These things all remind the cats of hunting.

There are lots of fun toys for cats.

This cat is sneaking up on something.

This girl and her cat are good friends.

LOTS OF LOVE!

Some cats like to be cuddled. They love to curl up on people's laps. Other cats are not so cuddly. But they still might like to be petted. Listen for their purring sound. A cat's purring lets you know it is happy!

This cat is happy— and sleepy!

NEEDS AND DANGERS

NEEDS:
- good food
- clean water
- a litter box
- a nice place to sleep
- toys
- grooming
- visits to the vet

DANGERS:
- running loose
- some kinds of houseplants
- household poisons
- getting stuck
- dogs that chase cats
- rubber bands, ribbons, or strings they can swallow

FUN FACTS

EYES:
Cats see well in the dark.

EARS:
Cats have very good hearing.

COAT:
Cats come in many colors. Their fur often has pretty patterns.

WHISKERS:
Cats' whiskers can feel the slightest touch.

TAIL:
When cats are upset, their tail twitches.

CLAWS:
Cats have very sharp claws. They keep them hidden when they are not using them.

GLOSSARY

curious (KYUR-ee-us) Curious means interested in things.

explore (ek-SPLOR) To explore is to go to new places or try new things.

grooming (GROO-ming) Grooming an animal is cleaning and brushing it.

litter (LIH-tur) Cat litter is made for places where cats go to the bathroom.

vet (VET) A vet is a doctor who takes care of animals. "Vet" is short for "veterinarian" (vet-rih-NAYR-ee-un).

TO FIND OUT MORE

BOOKS:

Ganeri, Anita. *Cats*. Chicago, IL: Heinemann Library, 2009.

Roca, Núria, and Rosa M. Curto. *Our New Cat*. Hauppauge, NY: Barron's Educational Series, 2006.

Zobel, Derek. *Caring for Your Cat*. Minneapolis, MN: Bellwether Media, 2011.

VIDEO/DVD:

Paws, Claws, Feathers & Fins: A Kid's Guide to Happy, Healthy Pets. Goldhil Learning Series (Video 1993, DVD 2005).

WEB SITES:

Visit our Web page for lots of links about pet care:
www.childsworld.com/links

Note to parents, teachers, and librarians: We routinely verify our Web links to make sure they are safe, active sites—so encourage your readers to check them out!

INDEX

ABOUT THE AUTHOR

Kathryn Stevens has authored and edited many books for young readers, including books on animals ranging from grizzly bears to fleas. She's a lifelong pet lover and currently cares for a big, huggable pet-therapy dog named Fudge.

24